Fight or Die!

A Key to Victorious Living

By Regina Gainer

ISBN 978-0-9712897-0-3

Additional copies of this book are available by mail. Send $10.00 each (includes tax and postage) to:

Regina Gainer
15 Williams Street
Bloomfield, New Jersey 07003
(973) 338-1350

Printed in the U.S.A. by
Morris Publishing
3212 East Highway 30
Kearney, NE 68847
(800) 650-7888

DEDICATION

I t is with love and gratitude that I dedicate this book to an army of heroes. They are the people who have inspired me because of their motivation to win their battles and because of their commitment to laying hold to victory. They are those who fight the good fight of faith and gain increased assurance that God will teach them new warfare tactics each time they are hit with a challenge.

To my husband, Pastor Nathan Gainer, who has been both supportive and prayerful in the completion of this book, I give my undying love. Honey, I will forever appreciate your love, protection and support in all of my endeavors. I love you for your patience and trust in the anointing upon my life.

To my brother, Pastor Charles W. Harris, Jr., who encouraged me and was persistent about my starting this project. Thank you for the design and donation of the book cover. I love you and appreciate your guidance.

To my mother, Maude Smith, who introduced me to God and to His greatness. I love you. You have always supported me prayerfully, financially and lovingly. Mommy, you are truly special to me.

About This Book

The author conveys practical wisdom that is founded on biblical principles providing the body of Christ with the ability to conquer life's dilemmas. The author shares insight and personal conviction for victorious living. She provides a key that will unlock doors as you travel your path to destiny. The contents of this book will encourage, provoke, and stimulate readers to be consistent warriors fighting the good fight of faith.

Pastor Charles W. Harris, Jr.
Bethel Church of Love and Praise
C.O.G.I.C.
Bloomfield, New Jersey

I came across this book at a time in my life when I had to make a decision whether to fight or die. Although I wasn't prepared to chose, I had to. This book gave me the knowledge, strength, and spiritual indignation to stand on my feet and begin to fight for my very life. And, like a personal trainer, the author motivated me to exercise my spiritual muscles. Soon, my confidence in waging spiritual warfare grew. I began to realize that with God on my side, there was no way I could lose.

Cinda Gaskin

*For the weapons
of our warfare are
not carnal, but
mighty
through God
to the pulling down
of strongholds.*

II Corinthians 10:4

CONTENTS

INTRODUCTION

D uring a dream one night, I saw what seemed to be demons fighting believers in a boxing ring. One by one, each believer would miss punches and strategic opportunities that would have easily put the demonic opponents away. The believers grew weary and began to faint. I yelled to them, "fight, fight, fight! Don't give up, fight, fight, fight!"

When I woke up, I felt tired and worn. From that time, the dream weighed heavily on my mind. I prayed and asked God to help me to understand the dream. He impressed upon my heart the words: "Tell my people that I have given them everything they need to win their battles. I have won the war for them. They can either FIGHT or DIE!"

The dream and the instruction that followed changed my life. Through my own personal battles, times when I have had to go toe to toe with Satan, and through helping others walk through their struggles, I have learned that we have to fight spiritually in order to win in every other dimension of life. I have observed that a great number of believers are not living the abundant life Jesus promised, but instead are living on the verge of giving up on God ever bringing victory into their lives. My heart aches when I see the frowned faces and slumped shoulders of depressed and even suicidal Christians who simply don't know how to win their battles against Satan.

No one can deny that life itself can sometimes be a hair-raising adventure. But it is in living through the struggles and through the onslaught of demonic attacks that most believers will learn how to fight. It is on these fierce battlefields that believers come to realize that the spiritual weapons they have received from God are powerfully effective, if they choose to use them. Also, each battle won brings with it a deposit of knowledge and wisdom they can share in helping others.

Though, at times, each bout appears worse than the last, an increased measure of anointing is released in the believer's life once he or she learns to fight with skill and courage. It's the kind of anointing that demands respect from Satan and causes him to retreat.

Chapter 1

THERE IS AN ENEMY

I nervously watched the clock on my classroom wall tick closer toward 3 p.m. That was the time I was slated to fight a giant. My giant was a 13-year-old girl known as "The Duke."

It was a bright June day, and the countdown toward summer vacation was well underway. When the school bell rang, a crowd quickly gathered outside to see what had been dubbed as "the fight of the year." As I walked into the schoolyard, I was shaking in my boots and could hear my heart pounding in my ears as I proceeded to get into position to fight.

"The Duke" was much bigger than I, both in weight and in height. The reputation as a bully had preceded her from the previous schools. This confrontation would determine if she would retain her title. As I sized up "The Duke," all I could hear in my ear was "fight or die." The words became louder and louder. All of a sudden, my courage arose and power burst forth in me that I had never felt before.

The totality of my 97-pound body began to manifest the physical strength of my heart's conviction. "I can win! I can win!" With one blow after another, my opponent was weakened and soon defeated. No longer did she boast in her victories. I had conquered my enemy and brought her to public shame.

One clear fact that stands out in my memory about this story is that I didn't choose "The Duke" as an enemy, but she had chosen me. Similarly, most believers know that Satan is the enemy of their souls, they often live in hope that they will never have to confront or fight him for themselves.

Satan, the Wicked One, the Adversary, the Accuser of the brethren, is the chief enemy of the believers. His main objective is to destroy mankind, God's prized creation. He hates the Most Holy God and His people who are created in his image and likeness. Our enemy comes in different forms and sizes, but his objective is always the same. Satan wants to destroy your faith and your effectiveness in leading others to Christ.

David faced a formidable enemy even before he was known as king of Israel. In fact, he was merely a shepherd boy when he faced Goliath. Let's consider the account in I Samuel 17:1-9.

"Now the Philistines gathered their forces for war and assembled at Socoh in Judah. They pitched came at Ephes Dammim, between Socoh and Azekah. Saul and the Israelites assembled and camped in the Valley of Elah and drew up their battle line to meet the Philistines.

There Is an Enemy

The Philistines occupied one hill and the Israelites another, with the valley between them. A champion names Goliath, who was from Gath, came out of the Philistine camp. He was over nine feet tall. He had a bronze helmet on his head and wore a coat of scale armor of bronze weighing five thousand shekels; on his legs he wore bronze greaves, and a bronze javelin was slung on his back. His spear shaft was like a weaver's rod, and its iron point weighed six hundred shekels. His shield bearer went ahead of him. Goliath stood and shouted to the ranks of Israel. "Why do you come out and line up for battle? Am I not a Philistine, and are you not the servants of Saul? Choose a man and have him come down to me. If he is able to fight and kill me, we will become your subjects; but if I overcome him and kill him, you will become our subjects and serve us."

Here, the Philistine army is the enemy, but Goliath is considered to be the archenemy. He is the chief, the selected and chosen head-hunter for the day. It is evident that he is confident in his ability to kill and gain victory over his enemy. In this case he considers Saul's army to be his enemy. He came against Israel spewing such penetrating intimidation that it paralyzed Saul's army.

David, the son of Jesse, looked beyond the giant's stature to see a God that was bigger then the giant that stood before him. David's faith, coupled with his experience, launched him into a one-on-one battle with the enemy. He was confident in his forthcoming victory which was part of his preparation to reign as king of Israel. Even as David stood alone, but yet not alone, there will be occasions when you too will have to fight a one-on-one battle against the enemy. Your strength and endurance will be based on the level of faith you have accumulated as a result of your relationship with God and your knowledge of the Word. Further, you must be convinced that God, the Great I AM, is living inside of you and causing your victory because He has made you more than a conqueror.

"No, in all these things we are more than conquerors through him who loved us."

Romans 8:37

A key to conquering the enemy is in defining the type of spirit that is coming against you. This can be accomplished by watching repeated incidents that occur in your life or in your family tree. For example, a spirit of rejection in your life could be the result of one of your parents' continued battle with rejection. This is what is known as a familiar spirit because it is familiar with your generational ties. In fact, the same spirits that fought against your forefathers will contend with you. Once you recognize this fact, you must prepare to Fight or Die! This is the time when you must face the enemies of your past generations and tell them that "The Buck Stops Here." Inform the enemy that you are a new creature in Christ, and that he (Satan) is already a defeated foe.

The enemy will even orchestrate family problems in order to cause believers to become weakened in their faith and intimacy with God. At one point in my ministry, the enemy began feeding me thoughts that led me to see my husband as an opponent. During that time, we seemed to have more disagreements than ever before. A wall was formed around my heart, creating bitterness and anger. There were times when his presence became uncomfortable for me. This was not normal because we had a tight relationship and have always enjoyed each other's company. On this note, we must realize that any situation or relationship that is good or will bring glory to our God, Satan will launch an attack. Just as our God is a jealous God, Satan is jealous also. Why? He can never regain and experience the intimate relationship he once had with Almighty God. He is doomed and will utterly be destroyed. His position in and with God is lost eternally.

One night in a service the Lord used a minister to speak to us. His words were, "You are not each others' enemy, the Devil is your enemy. Don't let him tell you that lie. Do not receive it, he wants you to accept it." He is the Father of lies and deception. You must know that a good marriage of two believers will never remain untouched by Satan. Favor, harmony and oneness with each other are not in his vocabulary. Hatred, jealousy and destruction are closer to what is produced from his devious character. There is no fair play in him, so stop feeling sorry for yourself and rise to the occasion. Pray a hedge of protection against the enemy's schemes and fight for your family, your marriage, and your life!

Chapter 2

RISE TO THE OCCASION

"Let no man's heart fail him because of this Philistine giant. I will go and fight him."

I Samuel 17:32

These words spoken by David to King Saul show David's courage despite his size and youth. Saul's reply was, "You are not to go out against this Philistine and fight him; you are only a boy, and he has been a fighting man from his youth." But David said to Saul, "Your servant has been keeping his father's sheep. When a lion or a bear came and carried off a sheep from the flock, I went after it, struck it and rescued the sheep from its mouth. When it turned on me, I seized it by its hair, struck it and killed it. Your servant has killed both the lion and the bear; this uncircumcised Philistine will be like one of them, because he has defied the armies of the living God. The Lord who delivered me from the paw of the lion and the paw of the bear will deliver me from the hand of this Philistine." Saul said to David, "Go and the Lord be with you." (I Samuel 17:33-37)

Like David, you must remind yourself of the things that God has done for you in the past to help build your courage when facing the enemy. Once you've conquered fear and put the enemy to flight in one area, beware that he is preparing an attack in another area.

Rise to the Occasion

Notice how David had to kill the lion and the bear. This was a previous confrontation that would be necessary for his forthcoming battle. So it is with the believer. While you are fighting to defeat one particular foe, a lust demon for example, the demon of destruction may be working on a plan aimed at devouring your family. You must simply rise to the occasion by first recognizing that you are in a fight and that the fight is for a reason. While accepting this as a Christian, you are automatically a target for the enemy who may initially sound intimidating. Do not lose heart because God has provided you with weapons that will strengthen you for every battle.

Prayer and fasting are two of your most effective weapons. These tools will help you fight fervently and will give you supernatural power and strength. Prayer and fasting will also help you to become sensitive to God and to hearing His voice. As you submit yourself to God in these two areas, He will reveal to you the "most wanted demon" in your life.

Through the anointing and power of prayer and fasting, God will also give you strategies that enable you to defeat the demon at large, no matter if it is being manifested in your family, on the job, in your finances, or in your health. As your confidence grows through the application of prayer and fasting, God will continuously teach you strategies and combination punches that will knock the enemy down and remove him out of that situation.

Fight or Die!

In Psalm 18:32-49 we read: *"It is God who arms me with strength and makes my way perfect. He makes my feet like the feet of a deer; he enables me to stand on the heights. He trains my hands for battle; my arms can bend a bow of bronze. You give me your shield of victory, and your right hand sustains me; you stoop down to make me great. You broaden the path beneath me, so that my ankles do not turn. I pursued my enemies and overtook them; I did not run back till they were destroyed. I crushed them so that they could not rise; they fell beneath my feet. You armed me with strength for battle; you made my enemies turn their backs in flight, and I destroyed my foes. They cried for help, but there was no one to save them to the Lord, but he did not answer. I beat them as fine dust borne on the wind; I poured them out like mud in the streets. You have delivered me from the attacks of the people; you have made me the head of nations; people I did not know are subject to me. As soon as they hear me, they obey me; foreigners cringe before me. They all lose heart; they come trembling from their strongholds. The Lord lives! Praise be to my Rock! Exalted be God my Savior! He is the God who avenges me, who subdues nations under me, who saves me from my enemies. You exalted me above my foes; from violent men you rescued me. Therefore I will praise you among the nations. O Lord; I will sing praises to your name."*

This psalm speaks of David's reliance on the Lord in helping him to rise victoriously from every battle. In 2 Samuel 8:14b, we read: "The Lord gave David victory wherever he went." David sought the Lord for each battle and needed a different strategy to win. Similarly, the Lord will give you victory in facing all the enemies in your path. However, you must seek God for the strategy He has designed for you.

From the onset of salvation in my life, I have experienced the ongoing battle of infirmities trying to invade my physical body. One incident that was more pronounced was a growth in my upper extremities. I was suffering with chronic reflux and was treating it with store bought remedies. Eventually, I saw a physician to confirm the growth which was on my esophagus. My doctor, appearing very concerned, scheduled me to see a gastroenterologist who would determine whether the growth was benign or malignant.

I began searching the Scriptures for verses relevant to my condition. This was the strategy God gave me. I began to quote one particular Scripture daily, and especially whenever fear began to knock at the door of my heart. I have to admit that doubt entered my mind at times when I undertook this strategy, but I remained consistent in my confession. Soon the Word that was in my mouth entered my spirit and eventually, it became a part of my spiritual exercise throughout each day. The supernatural operation began to take place.

Many times when the enemy threatens us, we want to grab hold of proven strategies, we pack up and fly to a Christian conference where the giants in the faith can pray for us. Or, we get other people to pray on our behalf. There's nothing wrong with these strategies, but in my case, there was no money for me to go to a conference at that time. I had to position myself to hold a private conference with the Father, the Word and the Holy Spirit. I did not depend on others' prayers. I simply put my plan into action and I soon heard God's voice saying, "Daughter, rise to the occasion for this is the time to fight or die!" I can show you my glory." I say "CAN" because some blessings and healings in MY plan for you are based on your faith and your fight.

Later, when I visited the gastroenterologist, he informed me that he intentionally looked a second time because he was sure of his diagnosis. To his surprise the growth was not there. He said to me, "who do you know?" I graciously shared my God with him. Hallelujah, the enemy was defeated! The strategy for the manifestation of my healing was—and I say "manifestation" because the healing was provided for me when Jesus died at Calvary, rose from the tomb and went into hell and took the keys from Satan and the curse of sickness was destroyed. All I needed was to believe that and FIGHT! My victory was manifested from doing the following:

1. I located my condition in the Word.

2. Memorized and quoted the scripture concerning my condition.

3. Let the Word become absorbed into my spirit by prayer, fasting and through faith in the person who spoke it.

4. Refused to waiver in my conviction.

5. Lived according to God's Holy Word.

6. Expected a victorious result by praising Him.

It is my prayer that you too will rise to the occasion and let God give you the victory no matter how the enemy is attacking. The Word of God gives you this promise:

"The Lord will grant that the enemies who rise up against you will be defeated before you. They will come at you from one direction but flee from you in seven."

Deuteronomy 28:7

Chapter 3

YOU ARE A CHOSEN VESSEL

"Jesse had seven of his sons pass before Samuel, but Samuel said to him, 'The Lord has not chosen these.' So he asked Jesse, 'Are these all the sons you have?' There is still the youngest,' Jesse answered, 'but he is tending the sheep.' Samuel said, 'Send for him; we will not sit down until he arrives.' So he sent and had him brought in. He was ruddy, with a fine appearance and handsome features. Then the Lord said, 'Rise and anoint him, he is the one.'"

I Samuel 16:10-12

E very family has a chosen vessel that will stand in the gap and fight with spiritual indignation and a determination to win. And like David, you are called to fight for your loved ones.

I can remember when we were a family of five—a husband, a wife and three children all living together. My husband and I reared our children in the fear and admonition of the Lord. We attended church regularly and were diligent in encouraging our children to get to know God and to serve Him faithfully. My husband and I worked in ministry and were faithful to our leader and to our church. In fact, our family traveled 50 miles to church. There were times when we had no car, and the five of us rode the bus for over an hour each way so that we could attend services. We even opened the church some Sunday mornings to clean it before services started. Because of our steadfast commitment to the ministry, the enemy knew he could not get us to be unfaithful to our God. His plan was to distract and destroy us through our children.

One night God visited me in a dream. In the dream, I saw armed soldiers outside my house. They were lurking in the doorways, peeking in windows, and trying to find a way to enter my house. Eventually, these soldiers entered through a bedroom window. Just moments before, I had escaped and found a place to hide. The enemy began attacking my children and then took them out of the house and led them to another land. When I woke up, cold and shaken, I asked God to reveal what that dream meant.

I sensed the Lord leading me into a season of warfare to destroy Satan's plan. Because I truly loved ministry work, I kept my hectic schedule and failed to make time to engage in serious warfare for my children. One by one their desires turned away from the things of God and toward the world and its allurements. Within a year and a half, both of my daughters left home six months apart. My son became ensnared by peer pressure that led him into trouble. The enemy used our children to bring shame and disappointment to my husband and me. He constantly spoke lies telling me that we had failed as parents.

Satan's purpose was to cause me to give up on my kids and bring public shame to God. It was difficult for me to engage in spiritual warfare while I was dealing with so much heartbreak and pain. Nonetheless, I realized that God had chosen me to be a warrior against Satan's plans to ultimately destroy my children. Brokenhearted, I repented to God for not heeding his instruction and became militant.

"Finally, be strong in the Lord and in his mighty power. Put on the full armor of God so that you can take your stand against the devil's schemes. For our struggle is not against the spiritual forces of evil in the heavenly realms. Therefore, put on the full armor of God, so that when the day of evil comes, you may be able to stand your ground, and after you have done everything, to stand."

Ephesians 6:10-13

As I pressed on in prayer, God soon healed me from the deep pain and I forgave myself. Again, I looked to the Word. I began warring with the spiritual armor God describes in Ephesians, Chapter Six. My prayers began to penetrate and turn my children's minds and hearts back toward God. Of course, it was not my prayers alone. My husband and the people of God were also praying that they would be delivered from the enemy's grip. But somehow I knew that God was dealing with me concerning spiritual warfare. I needed to see the power of my prayers. Many believers, because of their dependency upon others and riding on their prayers, miss the experience and joy of seeing God's power in another dimension. By living in this realm you can become limited as to how far you will extend yourself and make yourself available to pray until you see results.

You Are a Chosen Vessel

There are times when a one sentence prayer will get the job done. Yes, and it is according to your faith. However, as you venture into greater warfare and battles the level of your prayer must mature. The word context changes and the fervency and passion intensifies, which means longevity in prayer may occur.

Like David, I was a worshipper who had been called to war. I would have been very happy living out my life by basking in God's presence and singing about His peace and joy. But my children's lives were at stake. With the same passion I had poured into worshipping God, I went after the enemy in prayer until he loosed his hold on my children. Like David, I pursued the enemy until I made my name known within the enemy's camp. I was so fervent in prayer and fasting, that I imagined the demons saying, "Oh no, there goes Regina again, praying and shaking the gates. She has determined to fight and not leave us alone!" I had become like David who had also established his name in the enemy's camp. He terrorized his enemy and it was published throughout the nation. The Goliath victory birthed and gave rise to future victories for David.

Today, my daughters have good jobs and are good mothers. Both are attending church and have received the Lord Jesus Christ. I expect their eldest brother to follow shortly. I am aware that the devil has not ceased in his efforts to destroy them, so I continue to war for their souls. I thank God that He fashioned me to become a warrior and He will do the same for you.

Fight or Die!

"When the men were returning home after David had killed the Philistine, the women came out from all the towns of Israel to meet King Saul with singing and dancing, with joyful songs and with tambourines and flutes. As they danced, they sang, 'Saul has slain his thousands, and David his tens of thousands.'"

I Samuel 18:6-7

Chapter 4

FIGHTING AGAINST PERVERSION

"But mark this: There will be terrible times in the last days. People will be lovers of themselves, lovers of money, boastful, proud, abusive, disobedient to their parents, ungrateful, unholy, without love, unforgiving, slanderous, without self-control, brutal, not lovers of the good, treacherous, rash, conceited, lovers of pleasure rather than lovers of God."

2 Timothy 3:1-4

E ver since the 1990s there has been a proliferation of perversion in America and throughout the world. Perversion can be defined as a deviation from what is considered right or good. The spirit of perversion that characterizes our nation today manifests itself in many forms. The legalization of homosexuality is only one example of how this spirit is increasing throughout our society. Further, Generation X, or people born between 1977 and 1997, have embraced perversion as part of their cultural and sexual privilege.

Surprisingly, these young people are the very ones likely to see the Second coming of Jesus. It looks far-fetched, but the warring Spirit that God has placed in His people will deliver even Generation X from the hands of the enemy. God's warriors, the church, will conquer and defeat the "Philistine giants" that face them. The church is not limited to adults who war in the spirit to win today's generation to Christ. There are also Holy Spirit-filled youth who are willing to fight until their peers come to know the truth of salvation through Jesus. There is a boldness that Generation X has that the former generation did not have. While I am not discrediting our spiritual forefathers, the spirit of perversion that exists today demands a new dimension of courage. They must exhibit the boldness to withstand perversion regardless of the form it takes.

Earlier I discussed having three children. In 1986, the last of four were born. This child was a miracle from God since medical doctors said I would never carry a baby. When this baby, a boy, was in my womb, I actually felt like he was boxing with someone. The pediatrician told me that he had the strength of three babies. The pregnancy was a long haul. The forces of darkness fought me day and night. I was tormented with dreams and fears that affected my health. This baby was a stubborn baby with a strong warlike spirit. I knew this before he came forth. Because he decided to turn around and go back up I had to experience a Caesarean birth.

As he grew, his natural strength allowed him to lift a larger child over his head and throw him several feet. We were amazed at his strength. Being his mother and through observation I knew that there was a child of a God-given purpose. We knew that one day he would be a terror to the enemy. Similarly, the youth of this generation will rise and fight the spirit of perversion by using their God-given supernatural strength. The Father will use their bold music, their in-your-face clothing style, their abrasive language, and other characteristics which He chooses to destroy the work of the enemy in their generation.

"Don't let any look down on you because you are young, but set an example for the believers in speech, in life, in love, in faith and in purity."
1 Timothy 4:12

Parents do not allow your hearts to fear or fail. It is easy to become discouraged when you begin to engage in spiritual warfare against the perverse spirits of today's generation. And as you war against them, these spirits will begin to work to intimidate you and destroy your faith. Whatever the cost, do not give up. God has a plan for our children and it is imperative that we insulate them with prayer so that they can withstand the offensive perversions they face.

Although the spirit of this world has captured many of our young people and caused them to accept the lies of Satan, they cannot escape the call of God on their lives. You are in a fight and God has armed you with His Spirit to help you rescue our youth from such abhorrent spiritual perversions as school violence, life-controlling drug addictions, and a sexual confusion.

Fight or Die!

"He who is the Glory of Israel does not lie or change his mind; for he is not a man, that he should change his mind."

I Samuel 15:29

As intercessors, we must call the anointing forth in their lives so that they can war with the evil spirits and tear down the forces they face. Just as David was anointed in his youth for purpose and destiny, the Father is raising up a generation that is anointed with strength and courage to turn this world around.

Discouragement will come and knock at your door. Fatigue will set in and your words may begin to sound weak and faithless. Nevertheless, discipline yourself with a slap and remember the battle is the Lord's. You MUST come against these spirits in the name of the Lord who has already won the WAR!

When David faced his giant, his faith was not in the sling or in the stone he used to slay him. His faith was in the Lord.

David said to the Philistine: *"You come against me with sword and spear and javelin, but I come against you in the name of the Lord Almighty, the God of the armies of Israel, who you have defied. This day the Lord will hand you over to me, and I'll strike you down and cut off your head. Today I will give the carcasses of the Philistine army to the birds of the air and the beasts of the earth, and the whole world will know that there is a God in Israel. All those gathered here will know that it is not by sword or spear that the Lord saves; for the battle is the Lord's, and he will give all of you into our hands."*

Pray and believe that God will deliver our young people from perversion. Take your position and fight so that they will not die!

Chapter 5

TRUST YOUR ARMOR

"Finally, be strong in the Lord and in his mighty power. Put on the full armor of God so that you can take your stand against the devil's schemes. For our struggle is not against flesh and blood, but against the rulers, against the authorities, against the powers of this dark world and against the spiritual forces of evil in the heavenly realms. Therefore, put on the full armor of God, so that when the day of evil comes, you may be able to stand your ground, and after you have done everything, to stand. Stand firm with the belt of truth buckled around your waist, with the breastplate of righteousness in place, and with your feet fitted with the readiness that comes from the gospel of peace. In addition to all this, take up the shield of faith, with which you can extinguish all the flaming arrows of the evil one. Take the helmet of salvation and the sword of the Spirit, which is the word of God. And pray in the spirit on all occasions with all kinds of prayers and requests. With this in mind, be alert and always keep on praying for all the saints."

Ephesians 6:10-18

Trust Your Armor

Many Christians wear an armor that they do not fully trust. They have the Word, they have the Holy Spirit, but they simply do not trust in God's provision of a spiritual armor to protect them from the tricks of Satan. They have a tendency to trust what they see through natural eye and not through the Word of God. Their vision has become blurred and stigmatized causing them to stumble and become doubtful of their ability to fight.

Imagine a woman who is wearing a dress that is three sizes too big. She has to pin, tuck, and work hard to give the dress a shape that complements her body. Now imagine her changing into a dress that's three sizes too small. She has to take shallow breaths because the dress is pinching her torso, and she dare not sit or bend. Similarly, in the spirit realm, you must be fit for battle with an armor that is appropriate for you. Your level of faith should match your level of spiritual growth the way your shoe size should match your feet. This is important if you are to stay in the fight and apply fresh strategies from God as you war against the enemy.

The fact remains, you must fight or die! And like any ill-fitting garment, adjustments can be made. You may need to replace negative thoughts if your "helmet of salvation" is to fit properly. In this case, you must dismiss every unproductive thought or mindset that opposes your obedience to the Lord Jesus Christ.

Fight or Die!

"The weapons we fight with are not the weapons of the world. On the contrary, they have divine power to demolish strongholds. We demolish arguments and every pretension that sets itself up against the knowledge of God, and we take captive every thought to make it obedient to Christ. And we will be ready to punish every act of disobedience, once your obedience is complete."

2 Corinthians 10:4-6

Like a seed takes to fertile soil, negative thoughts can settle into your mind and begin to take root. As these thoughts grow, they become dominant and soon begin to set up a kingdom in your mind. In turn, this process will affect your "breastplate of righteousness," which protects your heart. Once the heart is infected by negative thoughts, it begins to produce sin. And sin, as you know, produces death.

"The mind of sinful man is death, but the mind controlled by the Spirit is life and peace; the sinful mind is hostile to God, it does not submit to God's law, nor can it do so. Those controlled by the sinful nature cannot please God."

Romans 8:6-8

"The acts of the sinful nature are obvious: sexual immorality, impurity and debauchery; idolatry and witchcraft; hatred, discord, jealousy, fits of rage, selfish

ambition, dissentions, factions and envy; drunkenness, orgies, and the like. I warn you, as I did before, that those who live like this will not inherit the kingdom of God."

Galatians 5:19-21

Having an armor you can trust depends greatly on your confidence in your relationship with God. Take an honest assessment of your daily devotions and intimacy with Him. If you fail to talk to your Father and spend time in His presence, your sense of discernment and spiritual awareness will become dull and lead to doubt and unbelief. These ugly twins produce fear, which is a red flag to the enemy that you are ready for the slaughter.

You must believe that every weapon that God has provided supersedes the weapons of Satan. And, you must believe that there is no weapon that is formed against you that can prosper (Isaiah 54:17). The weapons of Satan are designed to abort the promises of God for your life. By quoting the promises of God, you begin to set up a spiritual fortress against the enemy's attacks on your mind. However, some of God's promises depend on our obedience to His Word and on our willingness to make use of the weapons God has given us.

Imagine a person who purchases a gun for protection, but does not understand how to use the gun. He could end up injured or dead because of this lack of understanding. Just at the moment when he should be using the weapon for protection, he becomes confused and the adversary gains control.

Understanding your spiritual armor begins with looking at Jesus. Note how each part of the believer's armor represents the characteristic of our Savior:

a. The helmet of salvation—Jesus is our salvation.
b. The breastplate of righteousness—He is our righteousness.
c. Having loins girded about with truth—Jesus is truth.
d. The shield of faith—Jesus is faith.
e. Having feet shod with the gospel of peace—Jesus is our peace, He is the Giver of peace and the Prince of Peace.

Being fully persuaded and confident in the wearing of your armor will position you for greater victories. It also deepens your intimacy with God which brings you into a oneness in Him, a oneness that says, "when you see me, you see Jesus."

Chapter 6

FAITHFULNESS

"After Saul returned from pursuing the Philistines, he was told, 'David is in the Desert of End Gendi.' So Saul took three thousand chosen men from all Israel and set out to look for David and his men near the Crags of the Wild Goats. He came to the sheep pens along the way; a cave was there, and Saul went in to relieve himself. David and his men were far back in the cave. The men said, 'This is the day the Lord spoke of when he said to you, 'I will give your enemy into your hands for you to deal with as you wish.' Then David crept up unnoticed and cut off a corner of Saul's robe. Afterward, David was conscience-stricken for having cut off a corner of his robe. He said to his men, 'The Lord forbid that I should do such a thing to my master, the Lord's anointed, or lift my hand against him; for he is the anointed of the Lord.' With these words David rebuked his men and did not allow them to attack Saul. And Saul left the cave and went his way."

I Samuel 24:1-7

Fight or Die!

David's faithfulness did not start with the Philistine giant' It started when he was a shepherd boy. His faithfulness was cultivated on those sheep fields and eventually manifested in his loyalty to King Saul who was seeking to kill him. Though faithful, we know that David was far from perfect. But even in his repentance to God after his sin with Bathsheba, he proved that his heart was aimed at pleasing the Father.

Imagine how the enemies of Israel would have reacted if David, the anointed king, had killed Saul, the sitting king. Temptation was probably tugging on David's heart when he gave up the chance to kill Saul, not once, but twice (I Samuel 26:1-11).

Such an act of blatant disloyalty would have fractured the armies of Israel and the enemy could have gained victory in the midst of Israel's confusion. David's faithfulness to God and to King Saul was actually a strategic weapon.

Like David, your faithfulness can be used as a weapon against the enemy's schemes. The faithfulness in your life will manifest itself as you pursue the calling God has placed on your life. Many believers have been blessed with gifts and talents that can be utilized in the Body of Christ. However, assuming a place of service, the seed of faithfulness must be present and visible. One way to exercise faithfulness is by submitting your gifts and talents to the local church where your pastor can properly position them.

Faithfulness

You may be in a church serving under a pastor who does not seem to recognize your gifting. He or she may have asked you to serve in a capacity that does not exhibit your strongest talents. I encourage you to remain faithful. Every aspect of ministry is battle against Satan. Whether you are serving as a sweeper in the house of God or, serving as Chairman of the Board of Elders, your faithfulness to your position is a weapon aimed to annihilate the enemy's plan.

The road of faithfulness is sometimes lonely and frustrating. You may feel that your gifts are being wasted as you wait for your pastor to acknowledge and use you based on your talent. By submitting these feelings to God you resist the devil's attempts to gain a stronghold in your mind. He is then unable to plant the seed of rebellion and discord in you and in the congregation.

David being destined for kingship, never ceased to be a purposeful person. Not only would his faithfulness bring him promotion, but it worked within him the fruit of patience. Faithfulness and patience are kindred. They must come together in the midst of adversity and trouble. There are circumstances and situations that will persist in longevity, all of which faithfulness is needed.

"Submit yourselves, then, to God. Resist the devil, and he will flee from you. Come near to God and he will come near to you. Wash your hands, you sinners, and purify your hearts, you double-minded. Grieve, mourn and wail. Change

your laughter to mourning and your joy to gloom. Humble yourselves before the Lord, and he will lift you up."

James 4:7

Our God is an all-knowing and all-seeing God. His faithfulness is beyond ours. Being a compassionate Father, He comes to our aid. The fact of the matter is that faithfulness cries out for opportunity. It must be busy about purpose and cannot remain idle. So, your feelings are very real, nevertheless, you must fight the enemy's attempts to use these feelings for his purposes so that you do not miss God's purpose in and for your life.

Your regular attendance to Bible study and services of spiritual edification will facilitate the growth of faithfulness in your spirit. The intake of the Word will war against every negative thought and action that is introduced to you. Remember that you are destined for VICTORY! Do not allow the enemy to destroy the hope that is within you. Take your position of faithfulness in every area of your life. You must make the decision to either Fight or Die!

"But you, man of God, flee from all this, and pursue righteousness, godliness, faith, love, endurance and gentleness. Fight the good fight of the faith. Take hold of the eternal life to which you were called when you made your good confession in the presence of many witnesses. In the sight of God, who gives life to everything, and of Christ Jesus, who while testifying before Pontius Pilate made the good confession, I charge you to keep this command without

Faithfulness

spot or blame until the appearing of our Lord Jesus Christ, which God will bring about in his own time-God, the blessed and only Ruler, the King of kings and Lord of lords, who alone is immortal and who lives in unapproachable light, who no one has seen or can see. To him be honor and might forever. Amen."

I Timothy 6:11-16

Prayer

Father, help me to understand and appreciate your faithfulness to me. It definitely is not because of my goodness and righteousness, but it stems from your agape love. Create in me a thirsting to be in pursuit of the responsibilities you have orchestrated for my life. In fulfilling them I become more affective in the upbuilding of the Kingdom of God. I realize that my faithfulness to you will demonstrate my love and integrity. Forgive me for any hesitation and slothfulness toward my Christian duties. From this day forth I will walk worthy of the vocation I have been called to and will honor you and obey you as you so desire. In Jesus Name, Amen.

Chapter 7

PROPHETIC BATTLE PLAN

T he victories that David would win after successfully killing the Philistine giant, would be of another dimension. Successfully winning them, David gains respect in Israel. They honor and praise him above Saul. Their women sang songs:

"Saul has slain his thousands, and David his ten thousands."

1 Samuel 18:7

Saul, the King, became very angry with David and continuously watched him with the intent to kill him. Who is the enemy here? Is it Saul? Not so, his name is JEALOUSY. Because of your past victories, jealousy has and will confront you. This jealousy will come from friends and for some of you, leaders who are in authority. It is because the anointing upon you and in you to win battles. However, you must remember that the individual is not your enemy—it is Satan. Therefore, this kind of battle will require the "wisdom" of God. Never once did David disrespect Saul his leader. The Bible says:

"So David went out wherever Saul sent him and behaved wisely."

1 Samuel 18:1a

Prophetic Battle Plan

Your disagreement and confrontation with leadership should not bring rebellion in your heart. It is at this time that the wisdom of God must be in operation. This necessary ingredient will bring peace where there is chaos and distress. When the distressing spirit came upon Saul, David was chosen to play skillfully upon the harp. The result was that the distressing spirit left him. On another occasion, when David played the harp in the presence of Saul, Saul threw a spear at him to kill him, but David escaped. Saul now fears David because not only is God with David, but David is full of wisdom.

The spirit of jealousy will be exposed. Being full of wisdom, your reaction to the matter will bring glory, praise and honor to God. Wisdom will open the door of escape when necessary. Wisdom will also hide you from the attacks that come from the person who is jealous of your victories. The wisdom of God will also love and even protect your leaders when they are attacked and operate out of frustration and stress. Furthermore, it can be the catalyst used to open their eyes to see more clearly the perfect will of God.

The Body of Christ is getting ready to experience another dimension of wisdom for battle. Not only did it come with salvation, but there is a measure that is coming with the "smeared on" anointing that is being released upon and in the believer to do battle.

Fight or Die!

O n November 10th at about 1:30 a.m., as I was preparing to speak before my congregation, the Lord spoke to me and said, "I am releasing an anointing for battle. My people have fought battles, some in their own strength. Some were won with a word and others were won with a song. Some were won by Me alone. Their past victories have prepared them for the battles ahead. These battles shall be unlike any they have experienced. They are more intense. They are strategically launched and skillfully planned by Satan. However, I am permitting them to come. It will fulfill my purpose and bring forth much fruit."

It is imperative that my people sensitize their ears to hear me and open their hearts to receive me and believe me. I cannot lie and what I say, I will do. Taking heed to my voice will be the key element to win. You ask me how will I know? You shall know through prayer. You shall know through my word. For when I am speaking to you directly from my "logos", I shall illuminate my word. It shall leap from the page into your spirit. My "rhema" word shall be personalized for you. It is important for you to be connected to people who engage in battle and have the same mind. People who want deliverance and people who want victories.

Be careful and be not deceived by uniformity. It is different from unity. You can wear the same clothes, talk the same talk, but yet not have the same mind. I shall sharpen your discernment for you shall need this gift.

Prophetic Battle Plan

My children, I am releasing unto you <u>an anointing to battle</u>. You shall feel it and you shall wear it. It shall be smeared upon you and it shall be visible to your enemy. My glory upon you shall confuse him and cause him to make fatal mistakes that will give you victory. Receive ye this <u>anointing to battle</u>. You have already won!

MY PRAYER

Dear Father:

   I thank you for your love and your Son, Jesus Christ, who has given me the ability to be an affective Christian. It is Your grace that sustains me and causes me to triumph. I bless you, adore you and worship you for your greatness and your awesome power which is proven over and over to be unconquerable. It reveals to me that I can do and conquer all things with you in my life.

   Father, it is my continued desire to be successful in my walk as a believer and to accomplish the goals you have set forth in my life. Most of all, to bring Glory and Honor to Your Name.

   Love and Adoration,

   Regina

NOTES